IMAGES OF WAR
RETREAT TO BERLIN

IMAGES OF WAR
RETREAT TO BERLIN

IAN BAXTER

Pen & Sword
MILITARY

First published in Great Britain in 2011 by
PEN & SWORD MILITARY
an imprint of
Pen & Sword Books Ltd,
47 Church Street, Barnsley,
South Yorkshire.
S70 2AS

ISBN 978-1-84884-380-6

A CIP catalogue record for this book is available
from the British Library

Typeset by Mac Style, Beverley, East Yorkshire
Printed and bound in Great Britain by CPI

Pen & Sword Books Ltd incorporates the imprints of
Pen & Sword Books Ltd incorporates the Imprints of Pen & Sword Aviation,
Pen & Sword Family History, Pen & Sword Maritime, Pen & Sword Military, Pen & Sword
Discovery, Wharncliffe Local History, Wharncliffe True Crime, Wharncliffe Transport,
Pen & Sword Select, Pen & Sword Military Classics, Leo Cooper, The Praetorian Press,
Remember When, Seaforth Publishing and Frontline Publishing

For a complete list of Pen & Sword titles please contact:
PEN & SWORD BOOKS LIMITED
47 Church Street, Barnsley, South Yorkshire, S70 2AS, England.
E-mail: enquiries@pen-and-sword.co.uk
Website: www.pen-and-sword.co.uk

Contents

Introduction   6
Assessment of the German Soldier mid-late 1944   7

Chapter 1: Defensive Battles in the East   8

Chapter 2: Action in Poland   28

Chapter 3: Collapse in the East   49

Chapter 4: Defence of the Reich   69

Chapter 5: Stemming the Russian Advance   91

Chapter 6: Last Defence Before Berlin   110

Appendix I: Hitler's 'Fortified Area' Order March 1944   123
Appendix II: A Typical German Infantry Regiment 1944   125
The Author   128

Introduction

Drawing on a superb collection of rare and unpublished photographs this latest book in the popular **Images of War** Series provides an absorbing insight into the last desperate year of the German Army. In dramatic detail it analyses the German retreat from the wastelands of the Eastern and Western Fronts into a bombed and devastated Third Reich to the very gates of Berlin. Accompanied by in-depth captions and text, the book shows how Army, Waffen-SS, Luftwaffe, Hitlerjugend, and Volkssturm personnel try and defend every yard of ground from the overwhelming enemy. As the final months of the war are played out the reader will learn how the Germans fought to the grim death in a drastic attempt to prevent what Hitler called the 'two-fold devastation of the Reich'. Despite the adverse situation in which the German Army was placed, soldiers continued right to the very end, holding their lines under the constant hammer blows of ground and air bombardments. Those German forces that were fortunate enough to survive the overwhelming ferocity of the enemy onslaught, gradually streamed back where they were compelled to fight on home soil until they were either destroyed and its remnants encircled, or were driven around a devastated Berlin.

Assessment of the German Soldier mid-late 1944

The last six months of 1944 for the German soldier on the Eastern Front were very gloomy. They had fought desperately to maintain cohesion and hold their meager positions that often saw thousands perish. By the summer of 1944 the German forces were holding a battle line more than 1,400 miles in overall length, which had been severely weakened by the over-whelming strength of the Red Army. To make matters worse during the first half of 1944 troop units were no longer being refitted with replacements to compensate for the large losses sustained. Supplies of equipment and ammunition too were so insufficient in some areas of the front that commanders were compelled to issue their men with rations. As a consequence many soldiers had become increasingly aware that they were in the final stages of the war in the East, and this included battle-hardened combatants. They had also realized that they were now fighting an enemy that was far superior to them. As a consequence in a number of sectors of the front soldiers were able to realistically access the war situation and this in turn managed to save the lives of many that would of normally been killed fighting to the last man.

In spite the adverse situation in which the German soldier was placed during their retreat in 1944, he was still strong and determined to fight with courage and skill. However, by the summer of 1944 the German soldier had expended considerable combat efforts lacking sufficient reconnaissance and the necessary support of tanks and heavy weapons to ensure any type of success. The Red Army had constantly outgunned them, and the Luftwaffe air support was almost non-existent. The short summer nights too had caused considerable problems for the men, for they only had a few hours of darkness in which to conceal their night marches and construction of field fortifications. Consequently, the front line soldier in the forward combat area was already continuously under fire from Russian artillery and aircraft. Ultimately, the German soldier in the summer of 1944 was ill prepared against any type of large-scale offensive. The infantry defensive positions relied upon sufficient infantry ammunition supply and the necessary support to ensure that they would able to hold their fortified areas. Without this, the German soldier was doomed. Commanders in the field were fully aware of the significant problems and the difficulties imposed by committing badly equipped soldiers to defend the depleted lines of defence. However, in the end, they had no other choice than to order their troops to fight with whatever they had at their disposal. Their commanders were resolute in trying to hold back their hated Red foe in order to prevent them from reaching the borders of the Reich, and then on to Berlin.

Chapter 1

Defensive Battles in the East

In spite the success of the Russian 1944 summer offensive code-named Operation Bagration which saw the complete collapse of Army Group Centre, the Red Army were still unable to break the dogged determination and resilience of the German soldier. However, they were dwarfed by Russian superiority and they could do nothing to alleviate the overall predicament that was increasingly festering itself along the entire battered and worn Eastern Front. What followed during the last weeks of July was a frantic attempt by the Germans to stem the rout of the Soviet drive into Poland. Army Group North Ukraine tried its best to contain its slender position on the River Bug, whilst remnants of Army Group Centre tied with all available resources to create a solid front line Kaunas-Bialystok-Brest and assemble what was left of its forces on both its flanks. But between Army Group Centre and Army Group North German positions were depleted. The mauled 3rd Panzer Army had been fighting continuously in the area and even managed to capture and secure a number of villages in the area. In late July it captured Schaulen and then advanced on Mitau. The 3rd Panzer Army ordered the 7th Panzer Division to press on further and attack the Soviet 6th Guards Tanks Army in the area south of Kovno. The operation was very risky, but the Panzerwaffe once again demonstrated their effectiveness on the battlefield. The 3rd Panzer Army desperately tried to hold Kovno, fearing that loosing this Russian province would ensure the collapse of the Baltic States. On 31 July the Red Army pushed forward using their newly won freedom of manoeuvre in the direction of the East Prussian border. Meanwhile the 6th Panzer Division block the route towards Griskabudis, whilst Panzergrenadier von Werthen blocked the south bank of the Memel near Zapyskis. A few days later the Red Army unleashed a considerable number of tanks either side of Nova where the 6th Panzer Division was operating. What followed was the battle of Kovno.

Although German commanders were fully aware of the fruitless attempts by its forces to establish a defensive line, troops followed instructions implicitly in a number of areas to halt the Soviet drive. Again and again soldiers together with Panzerjäger and Panzer units fought to the death. In Latvia Bagramyan's 1st Baltic Front had meanwhile broken through to the Gulf of Riga, totally isolating Army Group North. From the west the 3rd Panzer Army bolstered by some 400 tanks and assault guns viciously counterattacked in the direction of Shauliya and Yelgava. The counterattack spearheaded by XXXX and XXXIX Panzer Corps was code-named 'Operation Doppelkopf'. Part of the German plan was to initially cut off the Soviet troops on the Baltic coast, and re-establish a tenuous 20-mile wide corridor connecting Army Groups Centre and North. The main objective of the attack was to re-take the key road-junction of Šiauliai, but Panzers soon ran into heavy defensive positions held grimly by the 1st Baltic Front. Despite its best efforts and the mauling of the 4th, 5th, 14th, and the once vaunted Grossdeutschland Panzer Divisions, they only made slow progress against the very strong and resilient Russian 51st, 2nd Guards and 5th Guards Tank Armies. By 20 August the German advance had stalled with heavy losses. But determined as ever to hold back the Red Army onslaught, another attack was launched. Within a matter of hours well sited Russian anti-tank gunners and tank crews brought the German Panzer attack to a flaming halt.

After a brief respite along the German front, the Soviets began preparing for the Baltic strategic offensive. On 14 September the German front lines in Latvia were brought under heavy systematic bombardment as Red Army troops were poised to attack on the Riga axis. The Panzerwaffe defending the area was aware of the geographical significance if the Baltic States were ever captured. Although the German defenders attempted to stall the massive Russian onslaught, by 15 September, the 3rd Baltic Front had ripped open and decimated much of the German lines in the east. From the south the Soviets were threatening the road to Riga, where the German X Corps had been heavily engaged in bitter fighting. Within a matter of days ten of the eighteen German divisions employed in the area around Riga to halt the Red Army had been reduced to a motley assorted collection of disjointed battle groups.

Heavily mauled German forces were now compelled to pull back west of Riga. As they prepared a new line of defence, the Soviets meanwhile were planning to launch another attack, this time southwards in preparation for a major drive towards Memel by the 1st Baltic Front. In just two weeks the 1st Baltic Front reached Memel while the 2nd and 3rd Baltic Fronts closed in on Riga. What was left of Army Group North, which amounted to some thirty-three divisions, was ordered to withdraw into the Courland peninsular and the Memel perimeter. Here valuable Panzer divisions that could have been used elsewhere on the front were needlessly ordered to hold out and become trapped so that they could tie down large parts of the 1st Baltic Front.

These were agonising moments for the German forces in the East. Despite the huge losses and lack of reserves many still remained resolute stemming the Soviet drive east, even if it meant giving ground and fighting in Poland – the last bastion of defence before the Reich.

Two machine gunners, one armed with an MG34 and the other with an MG42, are seen here departing from the entrance of their dugout. This photograph was taken on the Panther Line in February 1944, during which time the front lines had been temporarily restored. Within a month the Red Army was once again threatening large areas of the line again.

Right: A well camouflaged squad leader armed with a 9mm MP38/40. The MP38/40 machine pistol was commonly called the 'Schmeisser'. He is also armed with a M1924 stick grenade and wears a pair of 6x30 field binoculars.

Opposite: Two photographs taken in sequence showing a StuG.III maintenance depot in 1944 with a late variant StuG.III. By 1944 the StuG.III had become a very popular assault gun on the battlefield and was massed produced in order to try and contain the enemy. The vehicles had initially provided crucial mobile fire support to the infantry, and also provided their worth as an invaluable anti-tank weapon. However, during 1944 as the Eastern Front receded further west the StuG was primary used as an anti-tank weapon, thus depriving the infantry of vital fire support.

A photograph showing a heavy MG34 machine gun on a sustained-fire mount during a training exercise in 1944. In battle conditions in open terrain the MG34 machine gun squad would use their sustained fire-mount to protect the flanks of the advancing rifle companies. However, in built-up areas the crews often had to operate forward with the rifle platoons and in light machine gun roles with bipods only. They were able to still sometimes take advantage of the situation and revert back to heavy machine gun role.

A Hummel self-propelled gun moving to the front during the spring or summer of 1944. This popular vehicle was very effective weapon in the Panzerwaffe. A total of 666 Hummel's were built until the programme was finally terminated in 1944.

Fallschirmjäger troops with their 8cm sGrW 34 mortar in preparation for a fire mission against an enemy target. Each battalion fielded six of these excellent 8cm sGrW 34 mortars, and they were widely used throughout the war.

A Wehrmacht soldier in a typical dugout on the Eastern Front. For additional camouflage he wears camouflage netting on his M1935 steel helmet. Often foliage was woven through the netting to conceal the soldier in undergrowth, or whilst moving from one position to another across fields and other vegetation.

Along large sectors of the front troops built strong points which comprised of a number of light and heavy MG34 and MG42 machine guns positions, anti-tank, artillery guns, and occasionally self-propelled guns. However, many of these defensive positions were often ill-equipped or thinly manned with not enough ammunition or supplies. In this photograph a Fallschirmjäger MG42 machine gun can be seen on its sustained fire-mount, protecting the flanks of a attacking rifle company during the winter of 1944.

An interesting view of an MG42 machine gunner looking through the telescopic sight for closer grouping over longer ranges. The MG42 proved its capabilities in both offensive and defensive actions. Its dependability was second to none and every unit of the German army was equipped with this weapon. By 1944 many units had became totally dependent on these weapons to hold back the attacking enemy.

Two photographs showing a Waffen-SS 2cm *Flakvierling* 38 being prepared for action. These quadruple-barreled self-propelled anti-aircraft guns demonstrated outstanding anti-aircraft capabilities. As the war dragged on in the east many of these weapons were also be being used against ground targets, which was also very effective.

An Sd.kfz.251 has halted at the side of a road during operations somewhere in western Russia in 1944. The Sd.Kfz.251 had become not just a halftrack intended to simply transport infantry to the edge of the battlefield, but also a fully-fledged fighting vehicle.

Grenadiers conversing prior to moving out. Note the soldier on the right with an egg hand grenade being carried on his cartridge pouch's. All three soldiers are wearing the reversible winter jackets grey side out.

Grenadiers stand beside a halftrack. Throughout the war on the Eastern Front the supply situation was exacerbated by the almost non-existence of proper roads throughout the Soviet Union. Halftracks and other tracked vehicles were utilized to help speed up the supply of ammunition and other equipment desperately required for the front. Even during the latter period of the war in the East the halftrack was still an essential vehicle for the troops.

A StuG.III displaying a very full coating of Zimmerit anti-magnetic mine paste. In spite of the numerous advantages of the assault guns, equipping the Panzer units with these vehicles did not blend well with the nature of the Panzer. Yet, because of the lack of tanks in the dwindling ranks of the Panzer divisions, the StuG.III was used alongside the Panzer until the end of the war.

A StuG.III advances through a field with infantry hitching a lift somewhere in Russia in 1944. Despite the StuG's proven tank-killing potential and its service on the battlefield, the vehicle gradually deprived the infantry of the vital fire support for which the assault gun was originally built, in order to supplement the massive losses in the Panzerwaffe.

An MG34 machine gun squad crosses a stretch of flooded water in a rubber inflatable boat. This light MG is being used from its bipod mount. With the bipod extended and the belt loaded, the machine gunner could effectively move the weapon quickly from one position to another and throw it to the ground and put it into operation, with deadly effect.

A signals post somewhere on the front line in 1944. Even by this late period of the war rapid transmission of orders via radio and the fast action taken in response to them were the keys to the success of the German Army maintaining its position cohesively on the front-line. The equipment issued to the signals units varied considerably from field telephone sets, to ten-line subscriber networks and teleprinter, as well as transmitters and receivers.

Grenadier can be seen in one of the many trenches that formed hundreds of miles of the German front in 1944 and 1945. The core of these defences mainly composed of MG34 and MG42 machine guns, flak and PaK guns backed by all available tanks and assault guns. However, much of the front lines by the second half of 1944 were thinly stretched and unable to hold back the enemy for any appreciable length of time.

From a dug-out position in 1944 two officers can be seen wearing the green splinter Army reversible camouflage winter uniform. Behind the soldiers are a pile of stick grenades and Panzerfausts.

A telephone relay post somewhere on the Eastern Front during the summer of 1944. These troops were known as Strippenzieher (line puller). There job was primarily to talk to platoon and battalion headquarters, which would have to relay messages from adjacent companies.

Two Grenadier armed with the deadly Panzerfaust confers with their comrades before resuming operations. During the last year of the war the Panzerfaust was used extensively to combat Russian armour. It was a handheld rocket-propelled grenade, which was effective at a range of about 90-feet.

A well dug-in battery of flak guns in action against enemy targets. During the latter half of the war, as heavier and more lethal Soviet armour was brought to bear against the German Army, German forces clamoured to obtain more flak guns that could deal with the increasing enemy threat. By the second half of 1944 flak guns were assigned ro dual-purpose roles in order to try and stem the overwhelming steel tracks of the T-34 tank.

Above, below and opposite top: Three photographs taken in sequence showing German troops withdrawing through a decimated Russian town during bitter fighting in the summer of 1944. A destroyed T-34 tank which has been knocked out of action highlights the ferocity of the fighting in the rubble-strewn street.

Infantrymen clad in their great coats and insulated suits white side out pause in the march with a sled. Two of the soldiers can be seen holding their mess kit, which probably suggests they have stopped for a rest and to eat what rations they have left. They all wear the woolen toque and their M1935 steel helmet is camouflaged with white canvas sheeting.

Troops pose for the camera in front of a 'Mule', better known as a Maultier. The Maultier was armed with a ten-tube 15cm Nebelwerfer 42 on the rear of a halftrack. A battery of these formidable weapons fought on the Eastern Front in 1944 and 1945 in a vain effort to prevent the Red Army consolidating their bridgeheads.

Waffen-SS troops in their distinctive reversibles take cover on the side of a hill during intensive fighting. Note the captured Russian PPSh machine gun complete with ammunition box. In the field, the PPSh was a durable, low-maintenance weapon that could fire 900 rounds/min. Some 6 million of these weapons were produced by the end of the war, and the Soviets would often equip whole regiments and even entire divisions with the weapon, giving them unmatched short-range firepower. The gun had proven such an effective weapon on the battlefield that both the Wehrmacht and Waffen-SS used captured stocks extensively throughout fighting on the Eastern Front.

A 2cm Flakvierling 38 quadruple self-propelled flak gun near the front lines during the summer of 1944 can be seen in action against an enemy target.

An 8.8cm flak gun opens fire during an attack against a Soviet ground target. Note the gun's limber positioned nearby. The limber was normally positioned like this in order for the crews to rapidly limber-up and re-position the gun.

An Sd.Kfz.10 has halted beside a river and is protecting the river against possible enemy aerial attack. This vehicle mounts a shielded Flak crew. Note the magazine containers on the drop sides. By 1944 both Wehrmacht and Waffen-SS mechanized formations were well-equipped with flak guns.

A Luftwaffe manned 2cm FlaK30 light aircraft gun mounted in a well structured timber position. The young gunner can be seen seated and poised at a moment's notice to bring this weapon into action against an enemy target.

A 10.5cm infantry gun positioned with its trail spades near a stationary halftrack in the summer of 1944. Throughout the war the 10.5cm gun provided both the Wehrmacht and Waffen-SS with a versatile, relatively mobile, base of fire.

The gunner of a 7.5cm le.IG18 prepares his weapon for action by looking through the optical view finder. These small, light, highly mobile infantry guns were more than capable of providing troops with vital offensive and defensive fire support, particularly when heavy artillery was unavailable.

Chapter 2

Action in Poland

Between June and September 1944 the Germans had sustained some one million casualties. To make good their losses many of the exhausted undermanned divisions were conscripted of old men and low-grade troops. The method of recruitment generally did not produce very good results. Not only were the number of recruits simply insufficient, but the enlistment of volunteers in to the German Army was beginning to show signs of strain and exhaustion. In the Panzerwaffe too many of the replacement crews did not have sufficient time to be properly trained and as a result losses soared. Lack of fuel, not enough spare parts, coupled with the lack of trained crews all played a major part in reducing the effectiveness of the Panzerwaffe in the final year of the war.

Yet despite this deficiency in men and equipment the German Army did manage to slow down the Russian drive in the East, if only temporarily. On the central sector of the Eastern Front the remnants of the once vaunted Army Group Centre had steadily withdrawn across the Polish border westwards in July 1944. Its exhausted troops had been forced back towards Kaunas, the Neman River and Bialystok. By early August the Red Army was advancing a wedge toward Warsaw. The XX Army Corps immediately deployed a battalion to the newly formed 4th Waffen-SS Corps, due to the fact that the forces of the Waffen-SS Panzer Division 'Totenkopf' had been given the dutiful task supporting the right flank of the 2nd Army in the direction of the Vistula. The Red Army were now preparing to establish a bridgehead across the Vistula to the west and hoped that a rapid drive on the Polish capital, Warsaw, would bring a quick conclusion to the war. As Soviet forces spearheaded their troops across the Polish border toward the Vistula they used extremely rapid mobile forces. By using the heavy motorization it relieved the physical responsibility of the infantry. In many areas east of the Vistula the Russians met almost no resistance. During their almost unhindered drive they were able to cross the Warsaw – Lukow – Brest and Warsaw – Siedlce rail lines and cut off the 2nd Army from the important supply rail lines. The capture of the rail lines severely delayed units of the 4th Panzer Division from receiving reinforcements and ammunition. Consequently, much of the ammunition had to be brought by road risking the support column from being attacked by Red Army fighter bombers that were prowling the skies.

The 4th Panzer Division had been given the role of trying to stem the advance of the Soviet 2nd Tank Army. The division was divided into two battle groups. In total they had 98 combat vehicles available for action, only 69 of which belonged to the division. During its first encounters with the enemy in Poland in early August the division only claimed limited successful engagements. Although that figure was soon to rise during the first week of battle, German losses were kept to a minimum but the strength of the combat units was down to only 2,325 men.

On 11 August, as Russian forces fought on the upper Vistula between Army Group Centre and Army Group North, what was left of the 4th Panzer Division were hurriedly transferred to the Courland peninsula for another defensive battle. In Poland the situation had become much grimmer for the Germans as the Soviets moved on Warsaw. The 4th, 2nd and 9th Armies were engaged in bitter fighting as units desperately tried to hold the Vistula line from the Russians and prevent them from penetrating into Warsaw. Repeatedly, formations from other sectors of the Polish front were moved and immediately inserted into the frontal sectors to help bolster the German infantry and armoured units defending in front of Warsaw. Elements of the 19th Panzer Division were one of a number of units brought up as reinforcements. Although the Germans stiffened the defence line east of the city it did not prevent heavy combat occurring around the suburbs of Praga. It was here in these suburbs nearly five years earlier that German infantry and Panzers were victoriously fighting against Polish forces during the invasion of Poland. Now they were fighting for their lives against hardened, well-equipped and bitter Russian troops. By 14 September Praga was finally captured by the Russians, and Red Army forces now directly sent their infantry and armour across the river and held considerable stretches of the riverfront. Undeterred by the Soviets German troops remained holding tenaciously the ground west of the capital and fought for every foot. A mass of infantry, mixed with the remnants of naval and Luftwaffe groups, supported the motorised columns, as they fought against innumerable numbers of Russian tanks. Many of the German armoured vehicles were festooned with camouflage, and wherever possible moved under the cover of trees, or the cover of night to avoid being attacked by the Red Army Air Force, which had almost total control of the air on the Eastern Front.

By September 1944 the whole position in Poland was on the point of disintegration. Action in Poland had been a grueling battle of attrition for those German units that had managed to escape from the slaughter. Fortunately for the surviving German forces, the Soviet offensive had now run out of momentum. The Red Army's troops were too exhausted, and their armoured vehicles were in great need of maintenance and repair. It seemed the Germans were spared from being driven out of Poland for the time being.

Eight photographs taken of Luftwaffe grenadiers and officers of what was known generally as the Hermann Göring Korps. The Korps is obviously undertaking training, probably in Poland in the summer of 1944. The photos also include a Parachute Armoured Corps comprised of an unidentified assault gun unit.

An artillery observation post showing a soldier wearing the German Army splinter pattern reversible jacket looking through a pair of 6x30 field binoculars.

Troops during a patrol advance along a row of trees during an early summer morning. The fog shrouds the area and gives the patrol much needed cover. All the soldiers are wearing the Zeltbahn waterproof cape in order to try and keep dry.

The crew of a 7.5cm PaK97/38 appear to be connecting their weapon to a prime during operations in Poland during the summer of 1944. Fighting in eastern Poland was bitter, and both Wehrmacht and Waffen-SS anti-tank units fought almost continuously to try and hold back the advancing Red Army.

An interesting photograph showing German troops walking along a road with captured Russian soldiers. The soldier leading the group is a member of the *Feldgendarmerie*. Once German forces had occupied an area various administrative organizations were moved in to the particular occupied zone of operations, and these included military policemen or *Feldgendarmerie*. Note the dull aluminum gorget plate suspended around the neck by a chain.

A Waffen-SS 7.5cm PaK40 have positioned their gun at the side of a road. Along the road various halftracks and lorries probably carrying additional supplies and ammunition can be seen.

Two Kleines Kettenkraftrad Sd.Kfz.2 halftracks pass a German defensive position in Poland. These small motorcycle halftracks were widely used during the war on the Eastern Front, especially in the last two years of the campaign. They were very versatile machines and often hauled trailers and laid cable communications.

Two photographs showing a 15cm Nebelwerfer 41 being prepared and its deadly six-barrelled rocket launchers being fired against an enemy target. This weapon fired 2.5kg shells that could be projected over a range of 7,000 metres. When fired the projectiles screamed through the air, causing the enemy to become unnerved by the noise. These fearsome weapons that caused extensive carnage at Kursk served in independent army rocket launcher battalions, and later in the war in regiments and brigades.

A tracked vehicle has halted in a field with a 7.5cm PaK40 on tow. Even by 1944 the PaK40 was still widely used by both the Wehrmacht and Waffen-SS with deadly effect. In the hands of well-trained anti-tank gunners these weapons were able to undertake sterling service in defensive operations in Poland, and were able to score sizable successes against the Red Army.

A typical defensive position on the Eastern Front in 1944. Along the front troops have dug slit trenches and set up their weapons in readiness for the advancing enemy. The front would have comprised of a number of heavy MG34 and 42 machine gun emplacements, along with anti-tank and anti-aircraft positions too. Often located in between these positions were tanks and assault guns. Behind the lines halftracks and other highly mobile vehicles carrying troops were regularly seen moving into position in readiness to support the lines against the advancing enemy.

During operations in Poland a 2cm Flakvierling 38 is seen mounted on what appears to be an 8-ton Sd.Kfz.7/1 halftrack. The vehicle is concealed in a sun flower field. The gunners have liberally applied some foliage over parts of the vehicle and gun shield to break up the gun and vehicle's distinctive shape from aerial observation.

From his cupola a crewman of a Nashorn tank destroyer smiles for the camera beneath the potent 8.8cm PaK43 duel anti-tank/anti-aircraft gun. The Nashorn, although more sparsely available by the summer of 1944, still proved to be a highly effective tank killer. It was replaced in late 1944 by the Jagdpanzer IV and Jagdpanther.

Five photographs showing the 8.8cm FlaK gun on the battlefield being utilized both against ground and aerial targets. By 1944, SS mechanized formations had become very well equipped with FlaK guns. A typical SS Panzer-Division during this period was equipped with 12 heavy 8.8cm flak pieces, while less well equipped SS grenadier and Gebirgsjäger divisions still only possessed one or two, or none at all.

Troops move a PaK gun into position during defensive operations in an unidentified Polish town in the summer of 1944. By 7 August the Soviet offensive finally came to a halt east of Warsaw. The German front in Poland now stretched some 420 miles and was manned by thirty-nine divisions and brigades.

Grenadiers march along a muddy road which has obviously seen a lot of heavy traffic. The majority of the soldiers are all wearing the green splinter pattern Army camouflage smocks. As with later version winter camouflage smocks these uniforms proved to be extremely comfortable and as a combat garment gave the wearer plenty of movement and freedom and at the same time plenty of concealment.

A column of transport vehicles more than likely carrying supplies, ammunition and soldiers to another position. A typical division comprised of literally dozens of various light and heavy support vehicles. These support vehicles were constantly needed to support all movement, whether it was in advance or even withdrawing.

Waffen-SS troops move a tree from the road in order to allow an Sd.Kfz.251 halftrack to pass. In Poland the Waffen-SS were ordered to defend Siedlice, Warsaw, and the Vistula south to Pulawy.

A Tiger.I advances along a road somewhere in Poland. Between August 1942 and September 1944, some 1354 Tigers were built. During this period, these vehicles constantly demonstrated both the lethalness of their 8.8cm guns and their invulnerability against Soviet anti-tank shells.

Panther rolling along a road through a destroyed town, destined for the front lines. By 1944 the disparity of armoured vehicles meant that Panzers like the Panther had to wage continuous defensive battles in order to wear down the enemy in a war of attrition.

The crew of a halftrack Sd.Kfz.251 rest on the edge of a Polish village near the Vistula River. Along the river the Germans were thinly stretched and understrength against a numerically superior foe.

On the Northern Front and engineers can be seen constructing a temporary road out of felled trees. Often in forested regions of Russia and Poland the ground was waterlogged and regularly hindered the movement of traffic. Engineers were therefore required to build temporary roadways so that light traffic could move more easily.

Troops withdraw to another line of defence during bitter defensive operations in Poland. By September 1944 the situation on the Eastern Front was dire for the Germans. Almost everywhere units were being overwhelmed and slowly forced back.

A Waffen-SS light MG34 machine gun position in a short slit-trench. The slit trench often provided a soldier adequate protection from enemy rifle or machine gun fire and offered good overall line of fire.

A Wehrmacht soldier lays a Teller mine on the edge of a forest as his unit withdraws. The Teller mine was a circular steel cased anti-tank blast mine used by the Germans throughout the war, and millions of them were produced during that period.

German troops pose for the camera with a captured T-34, which was designated by the Germans as a Panzerkampfwagen T-34. Large number of T-34 tanks was captured and pressed into service by the Wehrmacht and Waffen-SS and were successful in a number of enemy engagements.

Panther has halted and the commander scours the countryside with a pair of field binoculars. During the bitter fighting in Poland the Panther was used extensively to thwart the sheer weight of the Russian drive. As German troops found themselves constantly becoming either encircled or cut off the Panthers were organized into special rescue units to relieve the trapped pockets of Germans. During the course of these daring rescue missions Panther crews fought with tenacity and courage, but time and time again the sheer weight of the Soviet army overwhelmed them. Although many Panthers were lost in action as a result of these brave rescue missions, it was the lack of fuel and ammunition that eventually forced these lethal machines to a standstill. (Michael Cremin)

Chapter 3

Collapse in the East

In spite the temporary lull in Poland, elsewhere on the Eastern Front the situation was dire. The 2nd Ukrainian Front had broken through powerful German defences supported by heavy armour, and had reached the Bulgarian border on 1 September. Within a week, Soviet troops reached the Yugoslav frontier. On 8 September, Bulgaria and Romania then declared war on Germany. Two weeks later on 23 September, Soviet forces arrived on the Hungarian border and immediately raced through the country for the Danube, finally reaching the river to the south of Budapest. Hitler placed the utmost importance on the defence of Hungary and ordered that his premier Waffen-SS divisions, including those vital forces positioned along the Vistula in Poland should be transferred to Hungary without delay.

Whilst IV SS Panzer Corps and two Panzergrenadier divisions were transferred to Army Group South to relieve Budapest, the Germans in Poland and in the Baltic States continued to rigidly commit everything it still had. Despite the dogged resistance, there was no coherent strategy, and any local counter-offensives were often blunted with severe losses. The Soviets possessed too many tanks, anti-tank guns and aircraft, and the Germans remained incapable of causing any serious losses or delay. Little in the way of reinforcements reached them, and those that were left holding a defensive position had already been forced into various *ad hoc* Panzer divisions that were simply thrown together with a handful of tanks and Panzergrenadiers. Much of these hastily formed formations were short-lived. The majority were either completely decimated in the fighting or had received such a mauling in battle they were reorganised into a different *ad hoc* formation under a new commander.

For the German soldier fighting for survival on the Eastern Front shortages of every kind was affecting all parts of the front. The lack of support vehicles and tanks were so critically low that by the end of the year the Germans were proposing mounting Panzergrendiers on bicycles.

As a result of their massive superiority the Russians continued pushing forward whilst German forces retreated through Poland to East Prussia. Along the Baltic coast too Soviet forces advanced crushing those German units which all that remained of the once mighty Army Group North. Hitler refused to allow the evacuation of 20 divisions – half a million men – which had been bypassed in the Courland peninsula. These heavy attacks eventually cut the vast territory formerly occupied by Germany in the northeast to a few small pockets of land surrounding three ports: Libau in Courland, Pillau in East Prussia and Danzig at the mouth of the Vistula. Here along the Baltic German defenders were reorganized as Army Group Centre in East Prussia and Army Group Kurland, the former Army Group North. All the German forces were understrength, and their defensive capabilities depended greatly on the old Prussian and Silesian fortresses of Breslau, Stettin, Küstrin, Folburg, Insterburg and Königsberg.

Massive though the Soviet force was in the Baltic, it was nothing compared to the forces available to the Red Army further south. There the winter offensive was to be a massive two-pronged attack through the rest of Poland, one leading along the Warsaw – Berlin axis commanded by Zhukov, with the other for Breslau under the command of General Konev.

A StuG.III Ausf.G inside a town somewhere on the Eastern front during late 1944. In spite the StuG's proven tank-killing potential and its service on the battlefield both in offensive and defensive roles, the increased use of the StuG as a anti-tank weapon deprived the infantry of the fire support for which the assault gun was originally built. By 1944, many StuGs were lost as a result.

Soldiers are seen advancing across a railway yard during operations in Poland in the late summer of 1944. Although the Russian advance through Poland by this time was relatively slow, the Germans were unquestionably stalling the inevitable defeat. Within months the German frontier would soon be reached.

Two soldiers rest in a field before resuming operations. One soldier wears the M1935 steel helmet, whilst his comrade is wearing the M1943 field cap introduced in mid-1943.

An SS FlaK gunner with his quadruple-barrelled self-propelled anti-aircraft gun. By 1944, mechanized formations were well equipped with flak guns. There were motorized flak battalions, with divisions being furnished with additional anti-aircraft platoons and companies in the Panzergrenadier, Panzer and artillery regiments. This flak gun was a formidable weapon and was more than capable of combating both low flying aircraft and ground targets. (Michael Cremin)

A soldier using an optical range finder to correct fire for the flak battery. Should rounds fall short or over target, his task was to advise the flak aimer on the corrections needed for the battery to hit the target. (Michael Cremin)

A solider attempts to quench his thirst on Russian vodka during his unit's withdrawal through Poland in the latter half of 1944. The German military situation by this time was dire. Continuously fighting against a numerically stronger opponent was now causing a severe lack of supplies, even in drinking water along some sectors of the front.

A Wehrmacht 10.5cm le FH 18/42 infantry gun crew in action somewhere on the Eastern Front during the winter of 1944. Throughout the war the 10.5cm gun provided both the Wehrmacht and Waffen-SS with a versatile, relatively mobile, base of fire.

An MG42 machine gun position sited next to a swamp somewhere in western Poland in the latter part of 1944. Although many sectors of the German front fought with fanatical resistance and held in a number of places, it came with a high price in men and material. However, the German soldier was still capable of meeting the highest standards, fighting courageously with self-sacrifice against massive numerical superiority.

Grenadiers rest along a roadside ditch in order to minimize enemy aerial attack. The soldiers are all wearing their Wehrmacht insulated winter suits. In the distance halted along a road are a number of armoured vehicles comprising mainly of halftracks.

An 8.8cm flak gun opens fire during a night time Soviet aerial attack on German positions. The gun's limber would often be positioned nearby in order for the crews to rapidly limber-up and re-position the gun.

Moving along a muddy road in western Poland is an Sd.Kfz.10 towing a 7.5cm PaK40. The halftrack is following one of the many horsedrawn carts pressed into service during the latter half of the war due to the lack of motor vehicles.

A Volkswagen Kubelwagen Type 82 has halted along a muddy road beside a halftrack. The Kubelwagen Type 82 featured a very reliable 4-cylinder horizontally opposed, air-cooled engine, capable of 23.5hp at 3000rpm and providing a top speed of 80km/h.

An Sd.Kfz.10 full of what appears to be wound Waffen-SS troops makes its way along a muddy road bound for a medical facility. By this period of the casualties had become such a major problem for both the Wehrmacht and Waffen-SS that many soldiers had to be left for collection whilst the main body of troops withdrew to another line of defence.

A column of Sd.Kfz.251s are seen withdrawing through a village in western Poland during the latter half of 1944. Note the spare wheels attached to the front of the halftracks for additional armoured protection. Halted in the mud are two late variant Pz.Kpfw.IVs with side skirts.

A tank crew discuss with the aid of a map the next course of direction for their armoured unit. Behind the crew is a stationary whitewashed Pz.Kpfw.IV. During the last year of the war the Pz.Kpfw.IV played a prominent role in the desperate attempt to halt the Soviet onslaught. Even though these powerful tanks were vastly outnumbered it was an ultimate credit to the Panzer divisions it served.

A column of Pz.Kpfw.IVs somewhere on the Eastern Front. The Pz.Kpfw.IV played a prominent role stemming the Soviet onslaught. Despite inferior numbers, the tank performed well in defensive operations, and achieved resounding success with the elite Waffen-SS divisions.

An interesting photograph showing an Sd.Kfz.2 crossing a frozen lake. This small tracked vehicle weighed a staggering 1.56-tons fully loaded, but was a very versatile machine. Its top road speed was 50-mph with a range of 156-miles.

Troops dig in along another line of defence. Halted next to them is an Sd.Kfz.10/4 with mounted FlaK gun. By 1944 both Wehrmacht and Waffen-SS mechanized formations were well-equipped with flak guns.

A halftrack tows an 8.8cm flak gun through the snow. The 8.8cm flak gun proved its worth during the last months of the war. Gun crews constantly utilized it against ground targets, and it was more than capable of disabling heavy Soviet armour.

Two photographs showing a well emplaced and camouflaged 8.8cm FlaK gun. The 8.8cm FlaK gun was often difficult to make out at long distances, especially when the crew whitewashed the weapon, which blended well with the winter surroundings. The gun fired a 9.4kg projectile, and its high velocity and flat trajectory made it a very accurate and effective weapon in both an anti-tank and anti-aircraft role.

A Panther has halted in the snow during winter operations in Poland in late 1944. The continuous fighting in the east gradually took its toll on tracks and other moving parts of the Panther, and those that were left fought a desperate defensive action all the way into Germany.

An interesting photograph showing a StuG.III Ausf.G during the winter of 1944. To maintain their speed, the accompanying infantry were often carried on the tanks and other armoured vehicles. When they ran into stiff opposition, they immediately dismounted to avoid taking heavy casualties.

Whitewashed StuG.III Ausf.Gs advance in the snow to meet the enemy. During the last two years of the war the StuG was gradually called upon for offensive and defensive fire support, where it was gradually embroiled in an anti-tank role trying to stem the might of the Red Army. During the last weeks of the war as fuel and spare parts became scarce many StuGs were either destroyed or simply abandoned by the crews.

A whitewashed staff car pulls alongside a whitewashed StuG.III.Ausf.G. The car carries the triangular pennant associated with that of a divisional commander. The StuG crew men both wear the reversible winter uniform white-side out.

A whitewashed Pz.Kpfw.IV has halted in the snow. Its driver can be seen chatting with two grenadiers wearing the familiar winter white smocks. The Pz.Kpfw.IV became the most popular Panzer in the Panzerwaffe and remained in production throughout the war. Originally the Pz.Kpfw.IV was designed as an infantry support tank, but soon proved to be so diverse and effective that it earned a unique offensive and defensive role on the battlefield.

A rifle company command post on the front line in western Poland in late 1944. The radio pack this soldier can be seen using was used for contact with the battalion command post.

With Soviet aircraft now ruling the skies in the East many German divisions had increased their anti-aircraft battalions, with each of them containing two or even three heavy batteries. In these two photographs an 8.8cm flak gun is shown complete with Schützschild (splinter shield) with its gun barrel in a horizontal position training the area against possible ground targets. In some sectors of the front, some units barely had enough Panzers to oppose the Russian armour and called upon flak battalions to halt the Red Army's attacks. During this later period many flak guns came to be assigned dual purposes, which involved adding an anti-tank role to their operational duties.

A truck carrying what appears to be food has halted on the edge of some woodland in the late winter of 1944. Rations and other supplies are already in the process of being unloaded.

An exhausted SS volunteer withdraws through a deserted Baltic village in late 1944 or early 1945. Conditions on the Eastern Front were miserable not only for the newest recruits but also for battle-hardened soldiers who had survived many months of bitter conflict against the Red Army.

Here SS volunteers are in action with a PaK40 during bitter fighting in the Baltic. The principal objective of the Red Army war was to crush the German forces in Poland, East Prussia and the Baltic States.

Support troops are photographed next to a whitewashed ammunition carrier during winter operations on the Eastern Front. One man is servicing the vehicle. This vehicle is armed with an MG34 with splinter shield.

Infantrymen wearing both the Army greatcoat and insulated winter suit white side out, assemble outside a building.

A halftrack is seen towing a PaK gun across a stream towards the front line. During the last winter on the Eastern Front both the Wehrmacht and Waffen-SS were falling back from one defence line to another, trying desperately to keep the Red Army from bursting through into Germany, and on to Berlin.

A Panzerwerfer unit during a fire mission in the snow in late 1944. This version comprised of an Sd.Kfz.4/1 and consisted of an armoured Maultier body with a ten-shot 15cm Nebelwerfer-Zehning 42 launcher mounted on the roof.

A group of soldiers pull a 3.7cm PaK35/36 up a slope in the snow. A typical infantry regiment controlled three infantry battalions, an infantry gun company with six 7.5cm l.IG18 and two 15cm s.IG33 guns, and an anti-tank company with twelve 3.7cm PaK35/36 guns.

Chapter 4

Defence of the Reich

On 12 January 1945, the Eastern Front erupted with a massive advance as Konev's offensive began with the 1st Ukrainian Front making deep wide-sweeping penetrations against hard-pressed German formations. The Russian offensive was delivered with so much weight and fury never before experienced on the Eastern Front. On the first day of the offensive the 4th Panzer Army took the full brunt of an artillery barrage followed by an armoured attack by the 1st Belorussian Front. It had total numerical superiority over the Germans with 7 to 1 in armour alone. The vast tide of the Red Army soon swallowed up the battlefield and by the end of the first day of the new offensive it had torn a huge breach over 20 miles wide in the Vistula front. The 4th Panzer Army had almost ceased to exist. Krakow was immediately threatened and German forces quickly manoeuvred to defend this ancient city.

On 14 January, Zhukov's 1st Belorrussian Front began its long awaited drive along the Warsaw-Berlin axis, striking out from the Vistula south of Warsaw. The city was quickly encircled and fell three days later. The frozen ground ensured rapid movement for the Russian tank crews, but in some areas these massive advances were halted for a time by the skilful dispositions of Panzers and supporting troops. Determinedly they held out in small groups of grenadiers supported by Panzers, until they too were annihilated or forced to fall back. What forces were available to try and stem the Red Army's advance to the frontiers of the Reich were pulled together into a new army group, 'Army Group Vistula'. Army Group Vistula was positioned behind the threatened front and consisted mainly of *Volkssturm* units and militia groups too young or old to serve in the regular army. Along this weak front, a number of volunteer SS units and *ad hoc* Panzer formations bolstered the understrength and under-trained forces, but they too had little with which to impede the Russian onslaught.

Over the next few days nothing could prevent the Soviet advance. On 25 January the Russians stood in front of Breslau and two days later the city of Memel fell. As German forces continued to fall back, they tried frantically to prevent the Red Army from bursting across the borders of the Reich and onto the River Oder, which was no more than 50 miles from the Reich capital, Berlin.

By early February 1945 German forces in the East had been driven back to the River Oder, the last bastion of defence before Berlin. Only three weeks earlier, the Eastern Front was still deep in Poland. Now Upper Silesia was lost; in East Prussia German forces were smashed to pieces; West Prussia and Pomerania were being defended by depleted troops thrown together, and the defence of the Oder was now being entrusted to exhausted armies that had been fighting defensive actions for months in Poland along the Vistula. What was left of these forces was supposed to hold the Oder front and fight to the death.

Along 200 miles of the defensive front remaining German divisions with handfuls of anti-tank and artillery guns were strung out along the front lines and were almost totally unprotected. A report noted that each division had to hold a frontage of approximately 20 miles. For every one mile of front some remaining regiments had one artillery piece, one heavy machine gun, two light machine guns and about 150 men. On every two and a half miles of front they had, in addition, one anti-tank gun. On every four miles they had one Panzer, and on every six miles one battalion. They were confronted by an enemy force made up of three tank armies consisting of thousands of tanks. Against this massive Soviet force was the German 9th, 4th Panzer and 17th Armies that fielded some 400,000 troops, 4,100 artillery pieces and 1,150 tanks. The 1st Belorussian and 1st Ukrainian Fronts had the Germans outnumbered on the average by 10:1 in tanks and self-propelled artillery, 9:1 in artillery and troops. In the First Belorussian Front alone this Russian Army had more infantry, tanks and artillery than the entire German Army on the Eastern Front.

In spite the overwhelming superiority German forces prepared their defensive positions along the Oder. On the night of 14 February the 11th SS Panzer Army actually mounted an attack, code-named Sonnenwende, and hit weak Russian units with its tanks. Although the daring Panzer attack caught the Russians by surprise, Sonnenwende was no more than a reprieve for the Germans. Along whole areas of the front the once-proud Panzer divisions had been reduced to skeletal formations on a stricken field. They were now not only vastly outnumbered but seriously lacked fuel supplies, lubricants and ammunition. When parts of the front caved in armoured formations were often forced to destroy their equipment, so nothing was left for the conquering enemy. The Germans no longer had the manpower, war plant or transportation to accomplish a proper build-up of forces on the Oder. Commanders could do little to compensate for the deficiencies, and in many sectors of the front they did not have any coherent planning in the event the defence of the river failed.

With every defeat and withdrawal came ever-increasing pressure on the commanders to exert harsher discipline on their weary men. The thought of fighting on German soil for the first time resulted in mixed feelings among the soldiers. Although the defence of the Reich automatically stirred emotional feelings to fight for their land, not all soldiers felt the same way. More and more young conscripts were showing signs that they did not want to die for a lost cause. Conditions on the Eastern Front were miserable not only for the newest recruits, but also for battle-hardened soldiers who had survived many months of bitter conflict against the Red Army. The cold harsh weather during February and March prevented the soldiers digging trenches more than a metre down. But the main problems that confronted the German forces during this period were shortages of ammunition, fuel and vehicles. Some vehicles in a division could only be used in an emergency and battery fire was strictly prohibited without permission from the commanding officer. The daily ration on average per division was for two shells per gun.

With such drastic restrictions of every kind, tens of thousands of under-nourished civilians, mostly women, alongside remaining slave labourers, were marched out to expend all their available energy to dig lines of anti-tank ditches. Most of the ditches were dug between the Vistula and Oder Rivers, as a secondary line of defence. However, German forces were now barely holding the wavering Vistula positions that ran some 175 miles from the Baltic coast to the juncture of the Oder and Neisse in Silesia. Most of the front was now held on the western bank of the Oder. In the north, the ancient city of Stettin, capital of Pomerania, and in the south, the town of Küstrin, were both vital holding points against the main Russian objective of the war – Berlin.

As the great Red Army drive gathered momentum, more towns and villages fell to the onrushing forces. Suicidal opposition from a few SS and Wehrmacht strong points bypassed in earlier attacks reduced buildings to blasted rubble. Everywhere it seemed the Germans were being constantly forced to retreat. Many isolated units spent hours or even days fighting a bloody defence. Russian soldiers frequently requested them to surrender and assured them that no harm would come to them if they did so. But despite this reassuring tone, most German troops continued to fight to the bitter end. To the German soldier in 1945 they were fighting an enemy that they not only despised, but also were terrified of. Many soldiers, especially those fighting in the ranks of the Waffen-SS decided that their fate would be met out on the battlefield. To them they would rather bleed fighting on the grasslands of Eastern Europe than surrender and be at the mercy of a Russian soldier.

The bulk of the German forces that were thrown together to defend the Reich and protect the route into Berlin were manned by many inexperienced training units. Some soldiers were so young that in their rations they had sweets instead of tobacco. All of them were ordered to stand and fight and not to abandon their positions. Terrified at the prospect of retreating, which would warrant almost certain execution if they did so, many reluctantly opted to bury themselves deep into a foxhole or bunker. Here they hoped the Soviet attackers would give them a chance to surrender, instead of burning them alive with flamethrowers or blowing them to pieces by hand grenade.

A 2cm Flakvierling 38 gunner has elevated his weapon for firing against an aerial target. The Flakvierling 38 combined four guns, and was served by eight men. These deadly guns were much respected by low-flying Russian airmen and were also particularly devastating against light vehicles, as well as troops caught in the open. The weapon also armed a variety of vehicles on self-propelled mounts where they could be moved from one part of the defensive line to another quickly and efficiently. (Michael Cremin)

From a dugout an 8cm Gr.W.34 can be seen in action. During the war the mortar had become the standard infantry support weapon giving the soldier valuable high explosive capability beyond the range of riles or grenades. Yet one of the major drawbacks was its accuracy. Even with an experienced mortar crew, it generally required 10 bombs to achieve a direct hit on one single target.

A soldier is reporting to his commanding officer, who is decorated with the Knight's Cross. This photograph was taken on the Baltic Front in late 1944. The soldiers wear both the splinter army insulated suit jacket and winter white reversible white side out.

Troops take cover in a trench during a lull in the fighting. The pile of Stg24 stick grenades indicates just how ferocious the fighting in the area could be. Note the unit leader armed with the 9mm MP38/40 machine pistol, one of the most effective submachine guns ever produced.

A whitewashed StuG.III Ausf.G halts inside a village somewhere on the Eastern Front. For the remaining StuGs that fought during the last months of the war, there had been hardly enough assault guns and other armour to stem the mighty Red Army, but even so courageous crews fought on ceaselessly trying to prolong the death throes of the Panzerwaffe.

An interesting photograph showing a column of Ausf.Gs halted on the outskirts of a village somewhere in the East. The leading vehicle has special *Ost* tracks fitted to the vehicle in order to give it better manoeuvrability across the often uneven and perilous terrain.

Troops are equipped with the 8cm sGrW 34 mortar in the snow. Each battalion fielded some six of these excellent 8cm sGrW 34 mortars, which could fire 15 projectiles per minute to a range of 2,625 yards. Aside from high-explosive and smoke bombs, this weapon also fired a 'bounding' bomb. It was very common for infantry, especially during intensive long periods of action, to fire their mortar from either trenches or dug-in positions where the mortar crew could also be protected from enemy fire. (Michael Cremin)

Winter warfare in late 1944; a well dug-in anti-tank crew with their deadly 7.5cm PaK40. The well concealed whitewashed gun presents a very small silhouette towards its front, and more likely to score sizable hits against advancing Red armour.

Soldiers pose for the camera in front of a whitewashed halftrack in the winter of 1944. Even by late 1944 the Germans were still fighting on foreign soil trying desperately to gain the initiative and throw the Red Army back from the remorseless drive on the German frontier.

A number of grenadiers have hitched a lift onboard a whitewashed StuG.III Ausf.G as its unit withdraws to another defence line. For the Panzerwaffe fighting for survival on the Eastern Front shortages of every kind were affecting most of the old and experienced assault gun units. (Michael Cremin)

A grenadier uses a knocked out assault gun as cover from heavy enemy fire. Throughout the later period of the war the StuG continued to provide its worth as an invaluable anti-tank weapon. Yet, in spite the huge losses, in a number of last ditch battles it showed its true capabilities as a tank killer.

A gunner can be seen with his 2cm FlaK gun during winter operations. The 2cm FlaK gun was a very effective weapon which was operated by only two men. Although these weapons were used extensively against aerial attack they were utilized against ground targets as well.

A rifle company, more than likely Estonian troops recruited into the German army in late 1944. They are all wearing the M1938 field cap and insulated suit jackets worn as appropriate for the local terrain and vegetation.

An interesting still film showing Hitlerjugend anti-aircraft assistants or helpers (Flakhelfer) being decorated by Luftwaffe commanders. Many Hitlerjugend helped in what was called 'the defence of the Fatherland'. In the background is their 2cm FlaK30 anti-aircraft gun.

A Waffen-SS Hauptsturmführer is being decorated with the Iron Cross 2nd Class whilst still on front line duties. Behind the newly decorated officer, note the discarded ammunition can which holds the three drum magazine for a Soviet 7.62mm DP light machine gun.

An officer holding the rank of an Oberst is seen talking to a Leutnant during an inspection parade in the Baltic in late 1944. Note the assortment of soldiers lined-up for the inspection wearing a variety of headgear including the M1943 and M1938 field cap. These are more than likely rear service personnel who were raised as emergency *ad hoc* units during the last months of the war. They often included wounded service men and foreign volunteers.

Estonian recruits on parade in front of their commanding officers in the winter of 1944. In order to bolster the dwindling forces in the East the Germans had conducted an extensive recruitment programme in Estonia, Latvia and Lithuania. Much of the draftees were dispirited, and their only motivation for fighting alongside the Germans was through fear of reprisals against their own people.

A Hummel advances along a road bound for the front. The Hummel mounted a standard 15cm heavy field howitzer in a lightly armoured fighting compartment built on the chassis of a Pz.Kpfw.III/IV. This heavy self-propelled gun carried 18 15cm rounds, and was a potent weapon against Soviet armour.

With Soviet aircraft now ruling the skies in the East many German divisions had increased their anti-aircraft battalions, with each of them containing two or even three heavy batteries. This photograph shows an 8.8cm flak gun complete with Schützschild (splinter shield). In some sectors of the front, some units barely had enough Panzers to oppose the Russian armour and called upon flak battalions to halt the Red Army's attacks.

Winter clad Nebelwerfer troops about to prepare their Nebelwerfer for a fire mission. The weapon was known as the NbW 41, which was a six-barreled rocket launcher mounted on a two-wheeled carriage. The rockets were fired one at a time, in a timed ripple, but the launcher had no capability to fire single rockets.

A gun crew are in the process of loading their 7.5cm PaK97/38 during a fire mission. The gun has been well emplaced next to stack straw and small trees in order to conceal it from the enemy.

As troops advance they come across what appears to be a knocked out Soviet 45mm M1937 anti-tank gun. The Germans used these captured guns throughout the war and named them 4.5cm PaK 184/1(r).

Waffen-SS troops wearing their winter whites march through the snow bound for the front line. These troops are part of a light MG42 machine gun squad. The MG42 had tremendous staying power against enemy infantry and soldiers took to continuously deploying their machine guns in the most advantageous offensive and defensive positions.

A unit prepares to move out. Note the troop leader armed with a 9mm MP38/40 machine-pistol slung over his back for ease of carriage during long marches. The MP38/40 machine pistol was commonly called the "Schmeisser".

A halftrack advances at speed across terrain flooded with water following a heavy downpour of rain. Even by the latter period of the war the Germans were still immensely hindered by the road network in the east. Heavy rain often turned a normal road into a quagmire making any movement very difficult, even for tracked vehicles.

Soldiers in late 1944 dressed in the familiar winter white reversibles are seen here surveying the terrain ahead trying to deduce the location of the enemy. At least four of the soldiers are wearing the fur covered cap. This was an unofficial style worn here in combination with the standard issue toque.

An MG34 squad march across a frozen plain to another line of defence. The soldiers are all wearing the special waterproof triangle camouflaged cape commonly known as the Zeltbahn. Even during the last months of the war many German troops still carried the Zeltbahn as part of their personal equipment. The Zeltbahn could be worn as a poncho over the field equipment, and it could also be worn buttoned up under the equipment as a form of camouflage.

A Russian soldier wearing the standard issue greatcoat and a fur covered cap can be seen manning a trench armed with a PPSh-41 sub-machine gun, which was the standard issue Soviet infantry gun used on the Eastern Front.

A Waffen-SS FlaK crew during operations on the Baltic Front. During 1944 a typical SS Panzer Division was authorized 80 towed and 40 self-propelled 2cm guns and 12 heavy 8.8cm flak pieces. Less well-equipped grenadier and Gebirgsjäger Divisions had 18 towed and 12 self-propelled 2cm guns.

Troops are receiving their meager rations from a makeshift mobile field kitchen in January 1945. By this time soldiers were becoming increasingly undernourished due to the severe lack of rations. The basic ration for the men was an army loaf and some stew or soup, which was often cold and unappetising.

Wehrmacht troops withdrawing across a muddy road. These soldiers comprised a new army group named 'Army Group Vistula', which was located between the Oder and Vistula rivers. These Wehrmacht troops together with Waffen-SS forces were supposed to prevent the Soviets from breaking through. However, the once mighty German Army was now suffering from an obvious lack of provisions and its strength was severely depleted. (Michael Cremin)

Panzergrenadiers wearing their distinctive winter reversibles white side-out have hitched a lift on board a whitewashed assault gun during the winter of 1944. Even as the war approached its end a number of assault gun units continued to spearhead the German armoured assault in a number of places. (Michael Cremin)

A group of Waffen-SS troops pose for the camera during a lull in the fighting in western Poland in 1944. The Waffen-SS were used extensively along the front line in order to prop up the crumbling front and temporarily stem the Red Army drive in many areas. As a result a huge amount of Waffen-SS soldiers were killed or injured.

SS soldiers pose for the camera with his quadruple-barrelled self-propelled anti-aircraft gun. By 1944, mechanized formations were well equipped with flak guns. There were motorized flak battalions, with divisions being furnished with additional anti-aircraft platoons and companies in the Panzergrenadier, Panzer and artillery regiments. This flak gun was a formidable weapon and was more than capable of combating both low flying aircraft and ground targets.

A halftrack negotiates a steep gradient during operations in the East in 1944. There were a variety of halftracks utilized on the Eastern Front to carry a wide variety of ordnance to the battlefront quickly and effectively.

A Waffen-SS patrol can be seen advancing through a shell-blasted forest somewhere in western Russia in late 1944. Note the leading soldier carrying a captured Russian 14.5cm PTRD-41 anti-tank rifle. The Germans referred to this weapon as the Panzerabwehrbuchse PzB 782(r).

Aerial attacks across the German front were merciless and often unceasing for many hours. The Soviet Air Force caused unprecedented amounts of destruction to German columns and defensive positions, from which many could never recover. Here in these two photographs is a Wehrmacht 2cm Flakvierling 38 crew.

Chapter 5

Stemming the Russian Advance

In the Baltic German forces were trying their utmost to stem the Russian advance in a desperate attempt to prevent Red Army forces from pushing down from the north into Germany and on to Berlin. The Germans were also clearly aware of the significance of losing their position in the Baltic sector. Not only would the coastal garrisons be cut off and eventually destroyed, but masses of civilian refugees would be prevented from escaping from those ports by sea. Terrified civilians eager to board the next ships to the Homeland queued night and day until the next vessel came in. They were so desperate to leave that they stood out in the open, enduring constant bombing and strafing by low-flying Russian aircraft, which were now unchallenged in the sky. Tens of thousands more civilians walked for days to reach congested ports along the Baltic like the ports of Pillau or the Kurische Nehrung in East Prussia. From here the boats would first transport the evacuees to Danzig or Gotenhafen and then from there to the more western parts of Germany. The crowding was so bad that a great number of them risked their lives by crossing the frozen east Baltic sea from East Prussia and the city of Danzig. At first light, the Russian Air Force swept over the columns of fleeing civilians. Women and children cowered as the pilots dropped their bombs, breaking the ice, and plunging hundreds of them into the freezing waters.

Even by the last weeks of March 1945, as Soviet troops spilled across Pomerania along the coast bypassing Danzig to the outskirts of Gotenhafen, the German Navy continued rescuing many refugees before the Red Army got to them first. German soldiers too, even remnants of elite Waffen-SS units, found themselves faced with a similar experience. Hundreds of dishevelled troops streamed out of East Prussia towards the coast, mingling with thousands of terrified women and children.

In the last week of March, as refugees fled from Danzig, the city came under direct bombardment. What followed was a bitter and bloody battle for the ancient Teutonic city. All over the Danzig savage and blood thirsty battles were fought. The stench of the fighting permeated every road and street. Along the main road leading to the centre hundreds of fires burned as buildings and armoured vehicles were struck by projectiles. Slowly and methodically the Russians began taking one district after another pushing back the defenders in a storm of fire and heavy infantry assaults. Whole areas were totally obliterated by tanks and artillery. Many Germans that were captured or wounded were executed on the spot and left suspended from the lamp posts as a warning to others. In parts of the city Volkssturm and Hitlerjugend supported by a mixture of Army and Panzer troops, managed to knock out a number of Russian tanks with Panzerfaust and Panzerschreck. But even these courageous fighters were no match for hardened soldiers that had fought their way bitterly through Russia to the gates of the Reich. German commanders tried their best to instil hope and determination in the poorly armed defenders, but district after district still fell to the Russian advance.

By 29 March those that had not been encircled or annihilated inside the city fled to mouth of the Vistula. Although the following day Danzig fell, resistance was not totally suppressed. A number of defiant groups that had been encircled and refused to capitulate fought on until they were annihilated.

Elsewhere along the Baltic coast the situation for the German Army was spiralling out of control, in spite of fanatical resistance. Inside the German city of Königsberg Hitler had ordered that the city be held at all costs. Five strong and determined German divisions comprised of some 130,000 troops manned an impressive array of defensive positions including fifteen 19th century forts interconnected by a maze of tunnels that could easily accommodate thousands of troops. German troops had made use of whatever they could muster to defend Königsberg from the Red Army. The five divisions defending the city were protected by three concentric rings of fortifications that surrounded the entire city. The outer ring of defences were reinforced by 12 forts outside the city, the middle ring in the outskirts and the inner city, and a single fortification that comprised of anti-tank defences, mines, and an assortment of barricades with a number of other bunker installations and forts.

Red Army commanders were well aware of the difficult task of breaking through the city defences and planned to rely heavily on systematic aerial and ground bombardment. Over the next few weeks hundreds of artillery pieces were drawn up and positioned by the Russians. In some areas there were some 250 guns per mile of front.

On 6 April 1945, the Russians finally attacked with a massive artillery barrage. Inside the fortress the Germans were assaulted from all sides but held their positions to the death. Throughout the afternoon of 6 April bitter fighting raged with both sides incurring such terrible casualties that the Russian assault broke-off.

The following day, on 7 April, Soviet troops once again attacked the city defences and this time several hundred soldiers armed with flamethrowers and hand grenades managed to cross the moat and enter the fortress where close quarter bloody fighting broke out. Whilst the troops bitterly engaged their German defenders the outer defences of the city were weakened by a massive frontal assault. Finally, the assault succeeded and much of the garrison surrendered. However, in some areas of Königsberg the Russians still met with fanatical resistance and had to reduce some parts of the city to rubble before the defenders either surrendered or were killed firing their last round.

German troops with captured Russian Maxim machine guns haul their booty to another line of defence. The leading soldier is armed with a captured Russian 14.5cm PTRD-41 anti-tank rifle, or the Panzerabwehrbuchse PzB 782(r).

A grenadier stealthily moves through a wooded area armed with the deadly Panzerfaust. The Panzerfaust literally meant armour or tank fist. The weapon was an inexpensive, recoilless German anti-tank weapon that was mass produced during the second half of the war. It comprised of a small, disposable preloaded launch tube which fired a high explosive anti-tank warhead, operated by one single soldier. Various models of the Panzerfaust remained in service throughout the latter part of the war.

A close-up view of two King Tiger tank men in 1945. Note the Zimmerit anti-magnetic mine paste on the turret. For additional armoured protection track links have been attached to the side of the turret.

Waffen-SS troops pose in front of an Sd.Kfz.251 halftrack. The Sd.Kfz.251 had become not just a halftrack intended to simply transport infantry to the edge of the battlefield, but also a fully-fledged fighting vehicle.

Two photographs showing one of the many knocked out Tiger and King Tigers during the last months of bitter fighting in 1945. Yet, in spite of the massive losses during this period, these vehicles constantly demonstrated both the lethalness of their 8.8cm guns and their invulnerability against Soviet anti-tank shells.

An SD.KFZ.10/4 with a mounted 2cm gun advances across a field with its crew on board. This piece combined four guns, and was served by eight men. These deadly guns were much respected by low-flying Russian airmen and were also particularly devastating against light vehicles, as well as troops caught in the open. The weapon also armed a variety of vehicles on self-propelled mounts where they could be moved from one part of the defensive line to another quickly and efficiently.

A 21cm Mrs18 being readied for a fire mission. This heavy mortar large-calibre gun had a range of almost 17 km, and its enormous range made the mortar a very effective artillery weapon. Although it was hindered by its weight of some 16.7 tons it remained in service until the end of the war. It was widely used destroying enemy fortifications and well dug-in positions.

Luftwaffe ground troops pose for the camera with a chicken they are preparing to cook. During the last months of the war thousands of Luftwaffe personnel were drafted in to fight on the ground alongside Wehrmacht and Waffen-SS forces.

German troops can be seen operating inside a destroyed German town during defensive operations. By this period of the war the Germans had become, like their enemy, masters in urban warfare.

At a forward post and signalmen can be seen with their small field telephone cable reels. This type of reel could be drawn by hand, or behind a bicycle. Often the cables were connected on poles to a radio truck (Funkkraftwagen). However, for speed on the battlefield signalmen frequently laid them on the round, but the cables were susceptible to breakages from passing traffic running over them.

A Wehrmacht soldier at a forward observation post surveys the battlefield through a pair of 6 × 30 field binoculars.

An Sd.Kfz.10 halftrack has halted along a narrow path. Engineers can be seen digging part of the embankment out with spades in order to widen the path for traffic. The Sd.Kfz.10 was designed primarily to tow light ordnance such as 2cm FlaK 30 or 38, 3.7cm PaK 36, 5cm PaK 38 and 7.5cm le.IG 18.

From a trench and a Luftwaffe soldier can be seen surveying the terrain through a pair of 6 × 30 field binoculars. Standing to his left is a soldier armed with the Mauser 7.9mm Kar98k carbine.

An interesting photograph taken during a 7.5cm PaK40 fire mission. One of the crew quickly hands the ammunition handler the characteristically long shells from the wicker protective casing, whilst another shell is already in the process of being fired.

A Waffen-SS 15cm s.IG33 artillery gun during a defensive action. A typical infantry regiment controlled three infantry battalions, an infantry gun company with six 7.5cm l.IG18 and two 15cm s.IG33 guns, and an anti-tank company with twelve 3.7cm PaK35/36 guns. The 15cm s.IG33 infantry gun was regarded as the workhorse piece, operated by specially trained infantrymen. (Michael Cremin)

Waffen-SS troops during a lull in the fighting. By this period of the war even the elite forces of the Waffen-SS could do little to prevent the mighty Red Army from reaching German territory and driving at breakneck speed towards the River Oder, the last bastion of defence before Berlin. (Michael Cremin)

Three photographs show a crew using the 7.5cm l.IG18. Each infantry regiment possessed its own artillery in the form of 7.5cm l.IG18 infantry guns. Each infantry gun company had six 7.5cm l.IG18s. Although the gun was one of the first post World War One weapons to be issued to the Wehrmacht, it undertook sterling service against the Soviet Army, even in the latter part of the war. (Michael Cremin)

A 2cm FlaK gun is being prepared for action. These quadruple-barreled self-propelled anti-aircraft guns demonstrated outstanding anti-aircraft capabilities. As the war dragged on in the east many of these weapons were also be being used against ground targets, which was also very effective.

A battery of Nebelwerfer has opened fire against an enemy position and their projectiles can be seen in the air. The Nebelwerfer was launched on a mobile carriage adapted from the 3.7cm PaK gun. It fired five or six rockets and was electrically fired over a period of 10 seconds. The weapon was designed to saturate a target with spin-stabilized smoke, explosive or gas rockets.

An 8cm GrW34 mortar and crew in the process of firing a projectile against an enemy target. There was a platoon of four 8cm mortars assigned to a grenadier battalion's machine gun company. The Germans found the mortar so effective that they often used many captured Soviet mortars and fired their own ammunition from them using German firing tables.

In a defensive position the crew of a 10.5cm field howitzer poses for the camera with their weapon. Combat experience showed that artillery support was of decisive importance in both defensive and offensive roles. The three light artillery battalions each had three four-gun batteries with 10.5cm howitzers. A battalion would usually be placed in direct support of an infantry regiment, but did not belong to the regiment. (Michael Cremin)

An artillery battery's observation post in action. Here the observer peers through his scissor binoculars. Acquiring targets across flat terrain was often much easier than hilly or mountainous terrain. Observation posts were normally located well forward of the infantry they supported, and it was essential that they were well dug-in and well concealed to ensure survival on the battlefield. (Michael Cremin)

Two photographs showing artillerymen plugging their ears the moment a 10.5cm artillery gun opens fire on an enemy position during defensive operations. It was primarily the artillery regiments that were given the task of destroying enemy positions and conducting counter-battery fire prior to an armoured assault. (Michael Cremin)

Two artillery crewmen rest during a lull in the fighting. They are sitting next to a pile of stacked 10.5cm shells still packed in their crates. Throughout the war the 10.5cm gun provided both the Wehrmacht and Waffen-SS with a versatile, relatively mobile, base of fire. (Michael Cremin)

Wehrmacht troops have disembarked from railways cars destined for the front lines during the last months of the war. Even during this late period of the war travelling by rail was often the quickest form of transportation. However, it was also the most dangerous, and as a consequence many thousands of troops were killed or injured by attacking enemy aircraft. (Michael Cremin)

An interesting photograph showing troops belonging to the famous Waffen-SS 'Wiking' Division. The division had suffered massive losses in the East and as a result had withdrawn through Poland where it took part in the defensive operations around Warsaw. (Michael Cremin)

It appears that this Waffen-SS PaK crew are heavily embroiled in a fire mission against an enemy target. As with many anti-tank gun crews they often concealed their weapon in order to wait for unsuspecting enemy armour to advance within good striking distance.

Wehrmacht troops scrutinize a map inside one of the many miles of trenches that were dug along the front lines on the Eastern Front. (Michael Cremin)

Waffen-SS troops rest during a lull in the fighting. Throughout the defensive fighting on the Eastern Front soldiers of the Waffen-SS fought courageously and continued to battle from one receding front to another. (Michael Cremin)

Chapter 6

Last Defence before Berlin

By early April the situation for Army Group North, now renamed Army of East Prussia, deteriorated further. Its forces were now hemmed in around the Bay of Danzig from Samland and Königsberg to the mouth of the Vistula. The remnants of two corps were given the task of holding positions north of Gotenhafen on the Hel peninsula. Hitler demanded that it be held at all costs. He instructed all forces in the Army of East Prussia and Army Group Kurland, to stay in the front, and then hold in order to draw the maximum enemy forces toward itself and hopefully away from the main Soviet drive on Berlin.

In the first two weeks of April as German forces tried to maintain their unstable position in the north the Red Army pulled together its forces into three powerful fronts with the main front being directed against Berlin. In the north the 2nd Belorussian Front was to cross the Oder north of Schwedt and strike toward Neustrelitz. Its thrust was intended to drive out the defending 3rd Panzer Army back against the coast and cover the advance toward Berlin on the north. German forces, however, were determined to try and hold their positions for as long as possible and prevent the Russians from taking possession of German territory. But in spite of dogged resistance in many places the Germans no longer had the man power, war plant or transportation to defend their positions effectively. The 3rd Panzer Army had 11 remaining divisions, whilst the 2nd Belorussian Front had 8 armies totalling 33 rifle divisions, 4 tank and mechanized corps, and 3 artillery divisions plus a mixture of artillery and rocket launcher brigades and regiments. The Germans were dwarfed by enemy superiority but continued to fight from one fixed position to another.

By mid-April the 2nd Belorussian Front had successfully pushed back the 3rd Panzer Army and had taken a bridgehead ten miles long above the city of Stettin. Inside Stettin the city had been turned into a fortress and was being defended by 'Fortress Division Stettin'. It was formed out of parts of the 3rd Panzer Army, and during its defensive battle it put up a staunch defence.

Elsewhere on the Eastern Front the Germans were trying their utmost to hold back the Russian drive. By April 1945 the atmosphere among the troops of Army Group Vistula became a mixture of terrible foreboding and despair as the Russians prepared to push forward on the River Oder. Here along the Oder and Neisse fronts the troops waited for the front to become engulfed by the greatest concentration of firepower ever amassed by the Russians. General Zhukov's 1st Belorussian Front and General Konev's 1st Ukrainian Front were preparing to attack German forces defending positions east of Berlin. For the attack the Red Army mustered some 2.5 million men, divided into four armies. They were supported by 41,600 guns and heavy mortars as well as 6,250 tanks and self-propelled guns.

At dawn on 16 April 1945, just thirty-eight miles east of the German capital above the swollen River Oder, red flares burst into the night sky, triggering a massive artillery barrage. For nearly an hour, an eruption of flame and smoke burst along the German front. Then, in the mud, smoke, and darkness, the avalanche broke. In an instant, General Zhukov's soldiers were compelled to stumble forward into action. As they surged forward, the artillery barrage remained in front of them, covering the area ahead.

Under the cover of darkness on the night of 15th, most German forward units had been moved back to a second line just before the expected Russian artillery barrage. In this second line, as the first rays of light prevailed across the front, soldiers waited for the advancing Russians. Along the entire front the 3rd and 9th Armies had fewer than 700 tanks and self-propelled guns. The largest division, the 25th Panzer, had just 79 such vehicles: the smallest unit had just two. Artillery too was equally spurse with only 744 guns. Ammunition and fuel were in a critical state of supply and reserves in some units were almost non-existent. Opposing the main Russian assault stood the 56th Panzer Corps. It was under the command of General Karl Weidling, known to his friends as 'smasher Karl'. Weidling had been given the awesome task of preventing the main Russian breakthrough in the area.

When the Soviet forces finally attacked during the early morning of 16 April, the Germans were ready to meet them on the Seelow Heights. From the top of the ridge, hundreds of German flak guns that had been hastily transferred from the Western Front poured a hurricane of fire into the enemy troops. All morning, shells and gunfire rained down on the Red Army, blunting their assault. By dusk the Russians, savagely mauled by the attack, fell back. It seemed the Red Army had underestimated the strength and determination of their enemy.

By the next day, the Russians had still not breached the German defences. But General Zhukov, with total disregard for casualties, was determined to batter the enemy into submission and ruthlessly bulldoze his way through. Slowly and systematically the Red Army began smashing through their opponents. Within hours hard-pressed and exhausted German troops were feeling the full brunt of the assault. Confusion soon swept the decimated lines. Soldiers who had fought doggedly from one fixed position to another were now seized with panic. The Battle for Berlin had now begun.

A Tiger tank halts in a decimated German town. During the war, some 1354 Tiger.I's were constructed. In spite of the military reversal on the Eastern Front, these vehicles constantly demonstrated both the lethalness of their 8.8cm guns and their invulnerability against Soviet anti-tank

German troops escort Russian POWs through an East German town following bitter fighting. The column of troops passes a stationary Pz.Kpfw.IV. Despite dogged resistance during the last desperate months of the war, the Panzerwaffe, lacking reinforcements, began to dramatically dwindle. As further losses multiplied, armour which had not been destroyed or encircled was forced to withdraw.

A flak crew in action with their quadruple-barrelled self-propelled anti-aircraft gun. Even by 1945, there were still a number of mechanized formations equipped with flak guns. This flak gun was a formidable weapon and was more than capable of combating both low-flying aircraft and ground targets.

On a road is a well camouflaged Sd.Kfz.10 with a quadruple mounted 2cm FlaK gun. Each of these flak guns had a practical rate of fire of 120 rounds-per-minute, with a maximum horizontal range of 4800 metres, which was particularly effective against both ground and aerial targets. A number of these mounted flak guns were used in the defence of Eastern Germany in a desperate attempt to help in the delay of the Russian onslaught. However, like so much of the German armour employed in the East, they were too few or dispersed to make any significant impact on the main Soviet operations which were already capturing or encircling many of the key towns and cities.

Young Wehrmacht troops smile for the camera as they march to the front. Along the front line to the east of Berlin the defences were made up of Volkssturm and Hitlerjugend supported by a mixture of Wehrmacht, Waffen-SS and Panzer troops. But even these courageous fighters were no match for hardened soldiers that had fought their way bitterly through Russia to the gates of the Reich. German commanders tried their best to instil hope and determination in the poorly armed defenders, but district after district still fell to the Russian advance.

During bitter defensive actions between the River Oder and Berlin thousands of Wehrmacht, Waffen-SS, Hitlerjugend and Volkssturm personnel were drafted in to defend their weak positions against the Red Army onslaught. In this photograph a Volkssturmmann has been paired off with a Wehrmacht soldier and is armed with the Panzerfaust 30. He wears an Italian helmet.

A unit marches off to the front. The soldier at the rear of the column is armed with the deadly Panzerfaust. As German forces fought to delay the enemy, the main bulk of the Red Army drive on Berlin began bypassing various pockets of resistance, where it fought a number of hard-pressed battles.

Wehrmacht recruits are given a quick lesson in the use of the Panzerfaust. By 1945 there was a dramatic increase in the loss of Russian tanks to the Panzerfaust and more than half of the tanks knocked out in combat were destroyed by Panzerfausts, or Panzerschrecks. The high loss became such a concern that the Red Army began installing spaced armour on their tanks. Each tank company was also assigned a platoon of infantry to protect them from infantry anti-tank weapons.

A commander gives his new recruits a lesson in using the standard German rifle with a gun sight. Well-trained snipers were a huge problem for both sides, and as a direct result they caused significant casualties, and often delayed a unit from moving until the sniper was taken out of action.

Commanders in the field are seen familiarizing themselves with the Panzerfaust. The oversize warhead was fitted into the front of the tube by an attached wooden tail stem with metal stabilizing fins. The warhead weighed 2.9 kilograms (6.4 lb) and contained 0.8 kilograms (1.8 lb) of a 50:50 mixture of TNT and hexogen explosives, and had armour penetration of 200 millimetres (7.9 in).

Two photographs showing troops armed with the lethal Panzerschreck or tank destroyer. The popular name given by the troops to this weapon was the Raketenpanzerbuchse or rocket tank rifle, abbreviated to RPzB. It was an 8.8.cm reusable anti-tank rocket launcher developed during the latter half of the war. Another popular nickname was Ofenrohr or stove pipe.

Two Wehrmacht soldiers armed with a Panzerfaust. This recoilless weapon consisted of a small, disposable preloaded launch tube firing a high explosive anti-tank warhead, operated by a single soldier. The Panzerfaust remained in service in various versions until the end of the war. The weapon often had warnings written in large red letters on the upper rear end of the tube, warning the user of the back blast. After firing, the tube was discarded, making the Panzerfaust the first disposable anti-tank weapon.

Grenadiers on the western bank of the Oder in March 1945. The solider on the left is using a Czech-made ZB vz/30 machine gun, a second-rate weapon that saw service with a variety of miscellaneous German formations up until the end of the war. Most of the front was held on the western bank of the Oder, less than 100 miles from Berlin. The Germans tried their best to form some kind of defensive position along the Oder, in spite of the badly depleted odd regiments and battalions that were thrown in to help strengthen the lines.

Two photographs showing German troops withdrawing through a decimated town somewhere in eastern Germany in 1945. In March 1945 there were two armies assigned to prevent the Russians from continuing their drive and capturing Berlin. On the northern wing was the 3rd Panzer Army under the command of General Hasso von Manteuffel. Eighty miles away in the south was General Theodor Busse and his 9th Army.

On the road to Berlin is a knocked out Jagdpanzer 38 (t) Hezter tank destroyer. This vehicle became the most advanced tank destroyer in the Panzerwaffe's arsenal. With its distinctive silhouetted armoured superstructure it carried a deadly 7.5cm PaK 39 L/48 gun on a specially widened Pz.Kpfw.38 (t) chassis. By the summer of 1944, it began joining the anti-tank battalions until the very end of the war.

A photograph taken the moment a Wehrmacht 8cm sGrW mortar crew go into action against an enemy target. In order to keep the mortar steady and accurate during firing two of the ammunition handlers would hold the tripod. This mortar earned a deadly reputation on the Eastern Front and was used extensively during the last battles before Berlin.

A column of dejected German PoWs march past a knocked out StuG.IV, probably in eastern Germany in March 1945. By February 1945 German forces in the East had been driven back to the River Oder, the last stronghold of defence before Berlin.

Soviet troops occupy a decimated town in eastern Germany in March 1945. A StuG.IV has been knocked out in street fighting. Although the last remaining Sturmgeschütz units saw extensive action, its success was limited and localized and did nothing to avert enemy operations.

An abandoned Jagdpanzer IV on a road outside Berlin in April 1945. With the drastic need for new armoured fighting vehicles more second generation tank destroyers were built. One such vehicle that came off the production line in 1944 was the Jagdpanzer IV. This vehicle built on the chassis of a Pz.Kpfw.IV weighed 28.5 tons and was nicknamed 'Guderian Ducks'. The vehicle was equal to any enemy tanks thanks to its potent 7.5cm gun. The Jagdpanzer saw extensive service in the east and with its reliability and well sloped thick frontal armour it became a highly efficient fighting vehicle, if only for a short period of time.

Appendix I

Hitler's 'Fortified Area' Order March 1944

The Führer
High Command of the Army

Führer Headquarters
8th March 1944

Führer Order No. 11

(Commandants of Fortified Areas and Battle Commandants) In view of various incidents, I issue the following orders:

1. A distinction will be made between 'Fortified Areas', each under a 'Fortified Area Commandant', and 'Local Strong points', each under a 'Battle Commandant'. The 'Fortified Areas' will fulfil the functions of fortresses in former historical times. They will ensure that the enemy does not occupy these areas of decisive operational importance. They will allow themselves to be surrounded, thereby holding down the largest possible number of enemy forces, and establishing conditions for successful counter-attacks. Local strong points deep in the battle area, which will be tenaciously defended in the event of enemy penetrations. By being included in the main line of battle they will act as a reserve of defence and, should the enemy break through, as hinges and corner stone's for the front, forming positions from which counter-attacks can be launched.

2. Each 'Fortified Area Commandant' should be a specially selected, hardened soldier, preferably of General's rank. The Army Group concerned will appoint him. Fortified Area commandants will be instructed to personally be responsible to the Commander-in-Chief of the Army Group. Fortified Area Commandants will pledge their honour as soldiers to carry out their duties to the last. Only the Commander-in-Chief of an Army Group in person may, with my approval, relieve the Fortified Area commandant duties, and perhaps order the surrender of the fortified area. Fortified Area Commandants are subordinate to the Commander of the Army Group, or Army, in whose sector the fortified area is situated. Further delegation of command to General officers commanding formations will not take place. Apart from the garrison and its security forces, all persons within a fortified area, or who have been collected there, are under the orders of the commandant, irrespective of whether they are soldiers or civilians, and without regard to their rank or appointment. The Fortified Area Commandant has the military rights and disciplinary powers of a commanding General. In the performance of duties he will have at his disposal mobile courts-martial and civilian courts. The Army Group concerned will appoint the staff

of Fortified Area Commandants. The Chiefs of Staff will be appointed by High Command of the Army, in accordance with suggestions made by the Army Group

3. The Garrison of a fortified area comprises: the security garrison, and the general garrison. The security garrison must be inside the fortified area at all time. Its strength will be laid down by Commander-in-Chief Army Group, and will be determined by the by the size of the area and the tasks to be fulfilled (preparation and completion of defences, holding the fortified area against raids or local attacks by the enemy). The general garrison must be made available to the Commandant of the fortified area in sufficient time for the men to have taken up defensive positions and be installed when a full-scale enemy threatens. Its strength will be laid down by the Commander-in-Chief Army Group, in accordance with the size of the fortified area and the task which is to be performed (total defence of the fortified area).

Signed: ADOLF HITLER

A Typical German Infantry Regiment 1944

Grenadier-Regiment 1944

Regiments-Stab
  Nachrichtenzug
  Pionierzug   6 x light MG34/42
  Reiter-oder Radfahrerzug   3 x light MG34/42
Grenadier-Bataillon (x2)
  Bataillons-Stab
  Schützen-Kompanie (x3)   16 x light MG, 2 x 8cm mortar
  Maschinengewehr-Komppanie   3 x light MG, 12 xheavy MG, 4 x 8cm mortar
  Leichte Infanterie Kolonne
Infanteriegeschütz-Kompanie   5 x light MG, 6 x 7.5cm inf gun
                             2 x 15cm inf gun
Panzerjäger-Kompanie   13 x light MG, 12 x 7.5cm AT gun
Regiments-Tross

Volksgrenadier-Regiment 1944/45

Volksgrenadier-Regiment 1944/45
Regiments-Stab
Stabs-Kompanie   10 x light MG34/42
Grenadier-Bataillon (x2)
  Bataillons-Stab
  Versorgungszug   2 x light MG34/42
Grenadier-Kompanie (x3)   9 x light MG
                         6 x 7.5cm inf gun, 6 x 8cm mortar
Infanteriegeschütz-Kompanie   5 x light MG, 4 x 7.5cm in gun, 8 x 12cm mortar
Panzerzerstorer-Kompanie   4 x light MG
                        54 x Panzerschreck

Regiment-Tross

Grenadier-Regiment 1945

Grenadier-Regiment, 1945
Regiments-Stab
Stabs-Kompanie   10 x light MG

Greandier-Bataillon (x2)
  Bataillons-Stab
  Versorgungszug   2 x light MG
  Grenadier-Kompanie (x3)   9 x light MG
  Schwere Kompanie   1 x light MG, 8 heavy MG, 4 x 7.5cm inf gun, 6 x 8cm
                                             Mortar

Schwere Kompanie   5 x light MG, 2 x 15cm inf gun, 8 x 12cm mortar
Panzerzerstorer-Kompanie   4 x light MG, 54 x Panzerschreck (+ 18 in reserve)
Regiments-Tross

Infantry Division 1944/45

By the last year of the war the infantry division had gone through a series of changes and had been modified and reorganised. The reconnaissance battalion for instance was removed and introduced with a bicycle mounted reconnaissance platoon within every regiment. The anti-tank battalion was more or less made motorised and consisted of an anti-tank company equipped with Jagdpanzer IVs, Hetzers or StuGs, which were organised into three platoons of 4 vehicles and an HQ section of 2 vehicles, a motorised anti-tank company of 12 x 7.5cm Pak 40 guns and a motorised flak company equipped with 12 x 2cm or 3.7cm flak guns. The engineer Battalion also took over the responsibility of the heavy weapons Company. It comprised of three engineer companies, each equipped with 2 x 81cm mortars, 2 x MGs and 6 portable flamethrowers. The heavy weapons in the engineer Battalion were normally mounted in trucks, but by 1944 they were predominately pulled by animal draught, whilst the troops would be mounted on bicycles.

At regimental level an anti-tank company was added. This consisted of a platoon equipped with 3 x 5cm Pak 38 guns and 2 platoons armed with Panzerfausts. Within the regiments, the infantry battalion were reduced in size to just two. A number of divisions in the field were attached with fusilier battalions and were structured identically to the new standard rifle battalion. The infantry battalions were equipped with 4 x 12cm heavy mortars, whilst the rifle companies heavy weapons platoon were equipped with 2 x 8.1cm mortars.

Panzergrenadier Division 1944/45

By 1944 many infantry divisions were re-designated as Panzergrenadier divisions. Although having an armoured designation, the Panzergrenadier division was still technically an infantry formation. However, unlike a normal infantry division there was a higher than usual attachment of armoured vehicles. A typical Panzergrenadier division had at least one battalion of infantry that were transported to the forward edge of the battlefield by Sd.kfz.251 halftracks, and various armoured support provided by its own StuG Battalion. A typical Panzergrenadier division normally composed an HQ company, a motorised engineer battalion and two Panzergrenadier regiments. Invariably a Panzergrenadier division had a StuG Battalion, which contained an HQ Platoon equipped with 3 StuGs and 3 StuG Companies. The StuG battalions were normally supported by a company comprising of a StuG platoon which was equipped with 4 x StuGs with 10.5cm guns, a flak platoon with 3 x quad 2cm guns mounted on Sd.Kfz.6 or 7 halftracks, an armoured engineer platoon with 5 x Sd.Kfz.250 halftracks, and a motorised signal platoon. Other support elements with the divisions comprised of the following:

Artillery Regiment 1944/45

3 x 2cm Flak Guns towed by a howitzer battalion
3 x 2cm Flak Guns
4 x 15cm sFH 18 Howitzers
4 x 10.5cm leFH 18 Howitzers
1 battery of 6 x Hummels
2 batteries of 6 x Wespes
1 Company of 14 x Jagdpanzers
15 x 7.5cm Pak 40 vehicle towed Guns
1 Company of 12 x Quad Flak 2cm Guns
2 Companies of 4 x 8.8cm Guns

Armoured Reconnaissance Battalion

4 Platoons of 4 x Sd.Kfz.231
MG Platoons of 4 x MG 34/42 (on sustained fire mounts)
3 x Rifle Platoons

Armoured Reconnaissance Battalion Support

2 x 7.5cm le IG 18 Guns
3 x 5cm Pak 38 Guns
1 x Engineer Platoon

Typical Panzer Division 1944/45

15,943 men

  91 × Panzer IV (7.5cm L/48 guns) medium tanks
  90 × Panther (7.5cm L/70 guns) medium tanks
  42 × Hetzer (7.5cm L/48 guns) tank destroyers
   9 × 15cm FH 18/40 towed howitzers
  18 × 10.5cm leF 18 towed howitzers
   6 × 15cm self-propelled sIG infantry guns
  12 × 7.5cm Pak 40 towed antitank guns
  36 × 5cm Pak39 towed antitank guns
  14 × 8.8cm Flak 36 towed antiaircraft guns
  12 × 3.7cm Flak 36 towed antiaircraft guns
  13 × 2cm towed antiaircraft guns
  32 × 7.5cm le. IG 37 and sIG 33 towed infantry guns
  80 x 8.1cm mortars
 570 x machineguns
  48 x Sd.Kfz 232 and 263 armored cars
1000 x trucks

The Author

Ian Baxter is a military historian who specialises in German twentieth century military history. He has written more than thirty books including Poland – The Eighteen Day Victory March, Panzers In North Africa, The Ardennes Offensive, The Western Campaign, The 12th SS Panzer-Division Hitlerjugend, The Waffen-SS on the Western Front, The Waffen-SS on the Eastern Front, The Red Army At Stalingrad, Elite German Forces of World War II, Armoured Warfare, German Tanks of War, Blitzkrieg, Panzer Divisions At War, Hitler's Panzers, German Armoured Vehicles of World War Two, Last Two Years of the Waffen-SS At War, German Soldier Uniforms and Insignia, German Guns of the Third Reich, Defeat to Retreat: The Last Years of the German Army At War 1943–1945, Operation Bagration – the Destruction of Army Group Centre, German Guns of the Third Reich, Rommel and the Afrika Korps, U-Boat War, and most recently The Sixth Army and the Road to Stalingrad. He has written over one hundred journal articles including Last days of Hitler, Wolf's Lair, Story of the V1 and V2 rocket programme, Secret Aircraft of World War Two, Rommel At Tobruk, Hitler's War With His Generals, Secret British Plans To Assassinate Hitler, SS At Arnhem, Hitlerjugend, Battle Of Caen 1944, Gebirgsjäger At War, Panzer Crews, Hitlerjugend Guerrillas, Last Battles in the East, Battle of Berlin, and many more. He has also reviewed numerous military studies for publication, supplied thousands of photographs and important documents to various publishers and film production companies worldwide, and lectures to various schools, colleges and universities throughout the United Kingdom and Ireland.